US and EU Cloud Computing Policy and Acceptance

For Regulated Entities

First Printing: 2017

ISBN-13:978-0-9985040-1-8
ISBN: 978-0-9985040-0-1
ISBN-10:0-9985040-1-7

Validated Quality Systems Publishing
1275 Bridle Path Dr
Lansdale PA 19446

www.validatedqualitysystems.com
www.vqsstaffing.com

US and EU Cloud Computing Policy and Acceptance

For Regulated Entities

Darral Addison

Validated Quality Systems Publishing

2017

Contents

Preface

The federal government is not in the business of developing new technologies, but they are in the business of facilitating them. If you are planning to develop computer-based products and services for regulated industries or would like to gain a better grasp on how IT policies are promulgated, then I strongly suggest you read this book.

This book will make plain which government agencies help promulgate policies that aid in the acceptance of Cloud and Computerized systems.

This book will help you understand how Cloud computing technology, design, and architecture are facilitated and protected by laws, regulations, and funding priorities. In the United States, the integrity, privacy, and security of medical and health records is a prime directive. In the European Community, personal privacy and data security are major factors that encourage the acceptance of cloud computing. Paying close attention to the spirit of the regulations, policies, codes, rules, and standards is key towards succeeding in the industry.

Even though policies, guidance, and interpretations from various agencies may echo similar definitions, it is important to understand those small distinctions governing each complementary framework. This book unveils the stakeholders and policy shakers who provide funding and drive public policy towards the acceptance of cloud and computer networks. Regulatory Agencies have developed a set of expectations for companies who develop and operate computer systems in regulated spaces. Understanding how these policies are promulgated help will uncover the IT requirements that drive industry activities.

Cloud Acceptance

Computing Evolution

Some see cloud computing as a new phenomenon. Cloud computing is not a new phenomenon, but it is a constantly evolving paradigm. Cloud computing has its beginnings in parallel, grid, and utility computing. Parallel and grid computing are the ancient forerunners to the cloud computing model. Grid and parallel computing provide a strong historical insight into the ways in which IT and compute muscle have evolved. For the most part, each evolving paradigm is invisible to the average person but has made tremendous contributions to our way of life.

Parallel computing consists of the simultaneous use of multiple computer or computing resources to solve computational problems. In this paradigm, multiple processors operate concurrently to solve problems. The problem is broken down into discrete parts and solved simultaneously by different processors. Parallel computing requires a lot of energy, control, and coordination between the various central processing units. 1

The migration from parallel to grid computing is more about the where than the how. Grid computing is spread out over multiple locations. Grid computing requires processing coordination between various computers.2 Grid computing builds upon the parallel computing paradigm by allowing individual systems to contribute to the compute muscle for solving problems. Grid computing allows scientists, developers, and administrators to take advantage of simultaneous processing over considerable distances. Grid computing leverages the resources of multiple systems to crunch out data. In this paradigm, hundreds of computers are linked together in a matrixed like formation similar to that of a grid. The network can utilize or build upon each system's processing power to solve a problem. Grid computing systems can be as simple as a collection of similar computers running mathematical and academic problems or as complex as inter-networked systems utilized for drug discovery, seismic analysis, or economic forecasting. Each system plays a particular role in solving the problem. Grid computing gave rise to a

---

[1] (Matloff, 2015)

[2] (Joseph, Fellenstein, and Moss, 2003)

new paradigm called utility computing, where computer resources have the ability to be metered out as a service. 3

"I value order above all."

Utility computing is another computing paradigm shift. Unlike grid computing, the utility computing model has moved capacity to solve problems from individual workstations to shared servers which are available through web browsers rather than personal computers. Utility computing allows users to have access to a wide range of multiple computer resources and services via the Internet. This is achieved at heightened speeds, and fast computational abilities, by sharing resources. You can link to your

---

[3] (Lutchman, 2003)

neighbor's server or local computer to retrieve or save files. In essence, you are sharing their resources. The best thing about these services is that they can be metered out. Utility computing allows entities to share applications online. Applications can be pushed out to your computer as a service online as needed. Companies can go online and push out resources and free up hard drive space, operating systems updates, and applications for less than it would cost to buy at a computer store. Administrators could whisk information to any location around the globe for archiving, backup, or general storage. The best thing about this new paradigm is that these services are always available as long as the grid is up. You would no longer have to get in your car and drive to the local computer store to buy an email application or use the postal service to mail out an application on a CD-ROM for patches and fixes. You can just log in online to any conventional browser and download the applications or push out the fixes. With the power behind utility computing, no one thought that life could get better.

Eventually, utility computing migrated from the laboratories, system administrators, and back-end processing for managing orders, inventory, and supply chain into the public sector. Utility computing evolved into cloud computing. Like utility computing, cloud computing is the ultimate share community where network-based subscriptions and applications are shared globally. The difference is that cloud computing migrated into being sold as a service. Services such as online music and movie streaming, online banking, educational, social networking services, and web-based emails are delivered metered out and marketed as a service to subscribers around the world.

Cloud computing is truly a global phenomenon. Not only can applications, software services, and storage resources be leveraged as an external or internal resource from your virtual office but they can also be accessed from anyplace in the world where there is network access. Services can be bought and sold to the general public. Big companies and environments that require high processing speeds, more hard drive storage, and bandwidth can lease these resources externally from service providers without having to invest in their existing infrastructure. Small companies can purchase business software packages to build a virtual office online without ever having to leave their living room. The cloud paradigm has opened up opportunities for various service providers to profit from the changing paradigm. Brokers, cloud service providers (CSPs), platform service providers (PSP), infrastructure providers, application service providers (ASPs), etc., and software development companies are just a few entities in a stream of solution providers working towards allowing businesses, consumers, and governments the ability to benefit from cloud computing. Purchasing software in the cloud eliminates the need for each entity (person, organization or business) to buy cumbersome hardware, mortar and brick locations, or unconfigurable software for their IT infrastructure. As long as each entity maintains their commitment to sharing or metering their resources, everyone can benefit. The cloud is only as good as each contributor.

Cloud computing technology not only gives you the ability to download applications and get access to information, but you can also leverage pay-as-you-go services. Most companies will allow you to pay for the services you need instead of having to sign a long-term contract or to commit to services you will seldom use. In the past, if you needed to increase your hard drive capacity you would back up your information, open up your computer and install your new drive or take your computer to the computer service center to install a new hard disk. Well, in the cloud paradigm, you only go online, find a company who will lease you their storage space and use the new location as an extended drive. Cloud computing gives users the ability to meter out compute power, data storage, bandwidth usage, and more. The result of combining technology resources yields decreased IT infrastructure. Cloud computing will allow you to minimize your IT infrastructure by outsourcing your need for more compute power, data storage, bandwidth usage, etc. Even though a portion of your network will be leveraged offsite, you can purchase pay-as-you-go security services online to ensure that only you can access your information. Cloud computing provides increased accessibility and availability of cloud resources. You can store information in the cloud, and retrieve it on-demand. Cloud computing has become the marvel of the world. As expected, cloud computing has emerged as one of the most powerful archetypes to date.

Cloud Space

Cloud computing has been described as a unique scalable architecture. While it is true that the information in the cloud rides on top of an underlying architecture, no one design defines the cloud. How the Cloud is structured is inconsequential. It does not matter if the architecture is expanded upon, redesigned or open to the public because the paradigm's existence is predicated upon the fact that you can combine different designs. The life of the cloud is based upon the assimilation of various structures to consume information.

Try not to look at cloud computing as just a collection of software and chip components. Also, do not consider it as a central entity that manages services and is controlling traffic and access from a central office. When cloud computing is referenced, it is a reference to everyone who takes part in services and activities in the infinite space. The cloud is not defined by schematics found in the hardware or software drawings. The cloud is a virtual community that comes to life. Cloud computing is a fluid paradigm. You can enter the cloud in many different ways. Everyone who willingly or unwillingly contributes information to the paradigm brings it to life. Everyone who has an electronic device adds to the cloud's existence. Bits and pieces of information that define who you are may reside in some entity's cloud. The cloud is an anomaly. It's defined by millions of people's desire to pull together resources and search for information.

Service Providers

Always remember that the cloud is a virtual community. Any one of the below entities can provide access to services to the cloud. You can enter the cloud in many different ways (laptop, telephone, cell phone, PDA, iPad, smartphones and tablet computers, wearable computers, smart watches, game consoles, portable media players, and more. Everyone who willingly or unwillingly contributes information to the paradigm brings the cloud to life. These contributions and solutions are available on demand. Anyone can subscribe to practically any service almost anywhere in the world.

Internet Service Provider (ISP)

Individuals and companies turn to an ISP when they need to have an Internet connection to access services in the cloud. From the Internet, you will get immediate access to thousands of applications and services such as online music and movies streaming, online banking, taxes, educational, social networking services, and web-based email. You can also get access to computing power, data storage, and bandwidth usage in the form of pay-as-you-go services.

Cloud Service Provider (CSP)

For companies that do not have the capital and expertise to build their cloud or that would like to utilize the services of a cloud supplier for infrastructure, or application services, they can purchase services from the CSP. CSPs are companies that offer dedicated and secure cloud infrastructure, or application services. These services are hosted in a data center that can be accessed over the Internet. Most service providers offer customers controlled and managed data center space with numerous connectivity options to house computing, storage, telecom and application server equipment. Depending on customer requirements, open racks, cabinets, or customized caged floor spaces are available across a global footprint of secure facilities. These facilities are designed to withstand major environmental incidents. 4

There is a plethora of service infrastructure supporting cloud activities. When we refer to these services, we use the xSP (ISP, ASP, MSP, HSP, SSP, WSP, NSP, etc.) service infrastructure acronym. Some of the service providers (SPs) by which we access the cloud include but aren't limited to:

- Internet Service Provider (ISP): Provides users with connection to the Internet
- Network Service Provider (NSP): Business or organization that sells bandwidth or network access by providing direct Internet backbone access to the Internet and usually access to its network access points

---

[4] **(Metheny, 2013)**

- Cloud Service Provider (CSP): A service provider that offers customers storage or software services available in the cloud
- Application Service Provider (ASP): Provides remote access to one or more computer applications
- Storage Service Provider (SSP): A company that provides computer storage space and related management to services
- Virtual IT Service Provider (VISP): Provides virtual services such as monitoring, reporting, remote management, backups, security and updates from a remote location

An ISP allows the customer to take advantage of online music and movie streaming. The CSP allows businesses to make use of Infrastructure as a Service (IaaS). IaaS allows equipment used to support your operations, such as storage, hardware, servers, and networking components, to be leased from a CSP. Likewise, Software as a Service (SaaS) allows users to take advantage of applications that are designed and hosted by software vendors around the globe and made available over the Internet. Platform as a Service (Paas) offers entities working on computer based development projects an excellent opportunity to work in a dedicated environment that can easily be leased by entities that need a virtual workspace. Whether you need a dedicated research or a stable and secure environment, numerous options can cater to your needs. Cloud computing is incredibly nimble. Consumers can jump, slip or slide into the fun. Moving into on-demand cloud services through mobile devices, smartphones, personal digital assistants, manifests, tablets, and various services in the cloud is a cinch. You can work anywhere because the cloud works everywhere.

US Government Computing Initiative

"We're going to shrink your department even more."

The Office of Management and Budget (OBM) chartered the Infrastructure Optimization Initiative (IOI) in 2006. The goal of the (IOI) is to develop strategic infrastructure initiatives to operate and maintain IT infrastructure efficiently and effectively. The IOI helps government agencies understand the underlying performance metrics when determining the effectiveness of particular services being offered by service providers. IOI wanted to compile and post the parameters in a central location so that government agencies can pick various services that are aligned with their mission. These metrics will help them achieve optimum performance. Performance metrics such as response time, peak capacity, throughput, demand management, availability, and downtime are just some of IOI performance metrics needing more clarity.

The performance level metrics were packed as a set of expectations for government agencies when entering into an agreement with a service provider. Before a government agency enters into a service level agreement (SLA) with a service provider, they could refer to the performance metrics as a gauge or a standard set of level service expectations for determining the reliability of the Service Provider. These service level expectations were packaged into what is now called Best Practices. IOI Best Practices define the set of performance standards expected to be used by governmental agencies when searching for a reliable service provider. Best Practices chronicles the level of the quality of service as well as the range of services of all of the parties in the service level agreement. It also defines the way that services are to be rendered and prioritized. According to IOI, the SLA defines relationships and sets expectations by describing the availability and delivery of services. If the levels of services are inadequate, compromised or if they cannot be rendered, the SLA can be referenced for mitigating contract disputes.

As new technology comes on line requiring new performance metrics, so will the need for redefining performance metrics in the SLA. The SLA must be crafted in such a static way even though standards are always changing. SLAs may have multiple stakeholders and therefore will not look alike. The SLA's existence is dependent on the types of services and products delivered over time. The multi-layer SLAs may include commitments with the service provider who has an agreement with the platform provider, who has an agreement with the infrastructure provider, who has an agreement with the application provider, who has an agreement with the software development company. IOI is responsible for optimizing government IT resources so that government agencies can focus on their mission priorities and not have to question if their CSP is providing them with a stable and reliable service.

IOI was later designated as the IT Infrastructure Line of Business (ITILOB).5 ITILOB's goal is to use a cloud computing technology platform that includes optimization strategies, performance metrics, and infrastructure tools for benchmarking federal IT data. In other words, ITILOB was assigned the responsibility to create an optimized, cost-effective collaborative Federal Government framework for all federal agencies. ITILOB spearheaded a government-wide study of end user systems and support, telecommunications, mainframe and server services. ITILOB established some expectations for cloud computing services. The result of the study was a written report. The report focused on encouraging the optimization, performance, efficiency, and effectiveness of the Federal Government's IT services. The report was so impactful that the Federal Chief Information Officer (CIO) Council identified cloud computing as a Federal IT priority. The CIO found it strategically necessary to form a CIO working group called Cloud Computing Executive Steering Committee (CCESC). 6

---

[5] (*Exhibit 300 Capital Asset Plan And Business Case Summary*)
[6] (Schlosser et al., 2009)

CCESC was established in March of 2009. CCESC estimated that over twenty billion of the Federal Government's eighty billion IT spending budget is a potential target for migration to cloud computing solutions.

CCESC's initiative is to drive innovation and encourage public partnerships that will foster the realization of a cloud computing framework. The upfront cost associated with the consolidation of IT resources is enormous. However, it is believed that the Federal Government can save as much as twenty billion dollars by utilizing a cloud platform. Twenty billion dollars is a staggering amount of money. The savings associated with re-engineering an architecture, migrating data, and streamlining applications is a game changer. CCESC wanted to transfer operating complexities that once were in the domain of administrators to be integrated into an automated framework that's outside the periphery of the users. The result will be a decreased infrastructure and an increased availability of on-demand cloud services. CCESC is comprised of four subgroups:

1. The Communications Subgroup is responsible for communicating the state of cloud computing within the Federal Government to federal agencies. It is responsible for conveying the cloud's functions and the purposes behind the functions.
2. The Operational Excellence Subgroup is responsible for providing assistance to federal agencies concerning cloud computing. It determines if the specifics within cloud computing have the potential of fitting into various agencies' operating framework and tries to uncover potential applications for cloud computing, and possible improvements.
3. The Standards Subgroup is responsible for developing standards and policies that will ensure that diverse systems and organizations can integrate procedures without negative consequences and ensure that the moving of data between cloud providers, whether public or private is accomplished with ease.
4. The Security Subgroup is responsible for ensuring that the cloud environment is secure. It ensures that security standards and controls are in place for housing data in the cloud.

In 2013, the Federal Government had over seven thousand data centers.7 In February 2010, the Federal Data Center Consolidation Initiative (FDCCI) was launched. The goal of FDCCI was to develop standards and policies, detailed consolidation plans, and technical roadmaps to eliminate no less than 800 federal data centers by 2015. This effort was to centralize the hosting of key applications and eliminate the need for infrastructure components that had become redundant. Ultimately, the effort reduced complexity within the federal IT environment.

---

[7] (S. Rept. 113-157 - The Federal Data Center Consolidation Act of 2013)

In 2011, the CIO was responsible for creating a Strategic Information Resource Management Plan for the federal government. The plan was centered on resourcing information and technology management activities for cloud computing to federal agencies. The CIO was responsible for ensuring that the federal agencies' movement to the cloud was adequately funded and in alignment with each agency's business strategy. The goal of this plan was to have each federal agency evaluate its current technology to see if cloud computing was a viable option. Federal agencies were tasked to investigate the benefits of cloud computing, develop a path and framework for establishing cloud computing, and apply resources for and develop roles and responsibilities to support cloud-based initiatives. Federal agencies were expected to investigate and invest in cloud computing technologies and adopt solutions that were cost-effective, reliable, and easy to integrate.

It's no secret that the CIO was well aware that operational efficiencies, for cloud computing communities, exceed the unnecessary cumbersome energy gulping data centers. Cloud computing communities are extremely elastic and have the potential to pool and reuse resources. Each community can achieve numerous deployment options that can make federal IT frameworks extremely agile and elastic while at the same time experience substantial reductions in cost. The cloud computing initiative is centered on providing a broad range of federal agencies' immediate access to scale up utilizing virtualized hardware and/or software infrastructure. Each agency will have computing resources at its disposal for achieving unparalleled scalability by design.

Most CSPs provide a suite of services from colocation to fully managed hosting. These services should include Privacy Level Agreements (PLAs) and SLAs from hardware to applications. CSPs provide an unlimited number of different services.

The General Services Administration (GSA) is an influential participant in the Federal Cloud Computing Initiative (FCCI).8 GSA is a key player in implementing projects and planning activities for the acquisition, deployment and utilization of cloud computing technology. The objective of the FCCI is to make cloud-computing services accessible and easy to procure for federal agencies. FCCI is also working towards increasing operational efficiencies, and program optimization between government agencies. Obscuring IT boundaries between federal agencies and realizing increased collaboration and data centralization within the Federal Government is a primary goal. The FCCI facilitated one of the first initiatives to create the Federal Government's definition of cloud computing.

The FCCI Executive Steering Committee, Advisory Council, and Working Groups are constantly working on identifying and addressing issues and obstacles to successful cloud computing implementation. FCCI's Executive Steering Committee's cloud computing mission statement is to reinforce, encourage, and expand the government-wide adoption of cost effective, green, and

---

[8] (KellyJOlson, 2011)

sustainable Federal cloud computing solutions. They are working towards establishing secure, easy to use, rapidly provisioned cloud IT services. These services include but are not limited to:

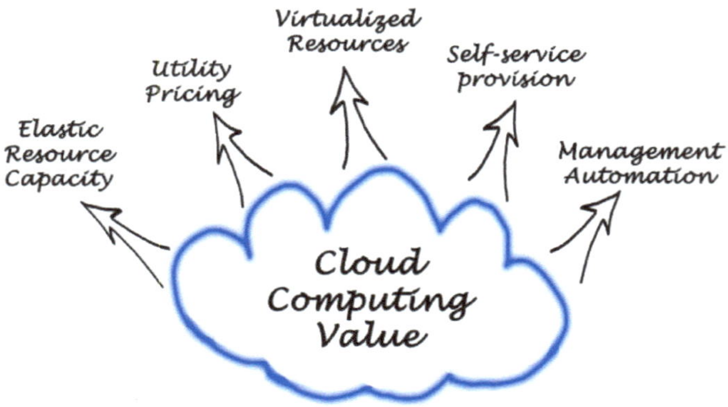

1. Developing a fast but yet simple acquisition and certification processes for cloud computing technology
2. Ensuring elasticity and smooth integration usage-based delivery of pooled computing resources
3. Ensuring business solutions are reusable and interoperable
4. Providing browser-based ubiquitous Internet access to services are accessible, always on and available

The GSA, the Department of Defense (DoD), the Department of Homeland Security (DHS), the National Institute of Standards and Technology (NIST), the OMB, and others work together to create the Federal Risk and Authorization Management Program (FedRAMP). 9

FedRAMP's goal is to ensure secure cloud systems. This program includes a government-wide, standardized approach to security assessments and ongoing continuous monitoring and authorizations of CSPs. FedRAMP works closely with cyber security and cloud experts from the NIST, GSA, DHS, DoD, NSA, and OMB to develop and implement security requirements for the Federal agency cloud-computing environment.10

1. NIST will lead and collaborate with federal, state, and local government agency CIOs, private-sector experts, and international bodies to identify and prioritize cloud computing standards and guidance
2. GSA will develop government-wide procurement vehicles and develop government-wide and cloud-based application solutions where needed
3. DHS will monitor operational security issues related to the cloud
4. DoD will accept and integrate a standardized approach to security assessments, authorizations and continuous monitoring for cloud products and services from FedRAMP.
5. The NSA will be responsible for evaluating their sourcing strategies to consider cloud computing solutions fully
6. Federal CIO Council will drive government-wide adoption of the cloud, identify next-generation cloud technologies, and share best practices and reusable example analyses and templates
7. The OMB will coordinate activities across governance bodies, set overall cloud-related priorities, and guide agencies

---

[9] (Program overview, no date)
[10] (Department of Homeland Security, Office of the Chief Procurement Officer, 2015)

The monitoring and authorization of CSPs save cost, time, and staff resources for federal agencies. It allows a one-time upfront assessment. The results of the evaluation are made available to all government institutions and businesses. A CSP's involvement in the standards program is optional. Any cloud service provider can apply to FedRAMP to be assessed. Once the assessment is completed, the CSP's quality of service, security controls, and security plan are published throughout the federal community. FedRAMP oversees the security testing that is conducted through a third party. If the CSP passes the assessment, FedRAMP makes a risk-based decision to determine whether to grant provisional authorization. Once permission is granted, federal agencies can petition FedRAMP for CSPs who are capable of meeting the requirements contained in the SLA, PLA, application-level, etc. Federal agencies can search FedRAMP to see if the providers' security credentials uphold risk clearance for hosting electronic data. Once authorization is granted, the CSP can be solicited for their services. The CSP is subject to ongoing security assessments.

NIST

NIST provides technical leadership for the nation's measurement and standards infrastructure for measurement phenomena. The Information Technology Laboratory (ITL) is one of the major research organizations within NIST.11 ITL acknowledges the immense short-term and long-term benefits by investing in cloud infrastructure. One of ITL's broader initiatives is to understand and define measurement phenomenon for science, technology, mathematics, and statistics. ITL develops test methods, reference data, proof of concept implementations, and technical analysis to advance the development and productive use of information technology. Additional responsibilities include the development of technical, physical, administrative, and management standards and

---

[11] (Hawes, 2016)

guidelines for the cost-effective security and privacy of sensitive unclassified information in the federal computing community. ITL's goal is to develop cost-effective guidelines that make financial sense, and that can be integrated or woven into the global IT fabric. The Computer Security Division of ITL, NIST, developed the definition of cloud computing. NIST's Special Publication defines cloud computing in very distinct terms.

> *Cloud Computing is a model for enabling convenient, on-demand network access to a shared pool of configurable computing resources (e.g., networks, servers, storage, applications, and services) that can be rapidly provisioned and released with minimal management effort or service provider interaction. This cloud model promotes availability and is composed of five essential characteristics, three service models, and four deployment models.*

Cloud technology is constantly evolving. The above definition is not designed to put cloud computing expectations in a box where the potential new paradigm must conform. The NIST definition merely serves as a baseline for gauging cloud services and deployment models. It is probably better to think of it as an explanation than an expectation. Cloud computing is not an out-of-the-box solution. Cloud computing technology is a trial and error process or a grand experiment. It is a risk-based experiment where the stakeholders map out how information will be collected, encrypted, and sent around the world.

Infrastructure needs may not necessarily be mapped out in a guideline or provided as an architectural realization that is defined in a book but may be a unique cloud hybrid that is aligned with your business goals. Take time to develop an assessment to find out what is expected from the cloud or how goals will be achieved. It is important that you experiment with various cloud deployment models to ensure that you have the right services and characteristics that suit your business objectives.

Essential Cloud Characteristics

CSPs are making numerous claims about the benefits of adopting cloud technology. Some of the claims can be easily seen, but for others, the benefits are not readily visible. For example, while many companies are experiencing tremendous savings in infrastructure reductions and an increase of on-demand products and services, others are hiring new staff to integrate their existing platform into the cloud fabric. What is good for the goose may not be good for the gander. Nevertheless, some of the most common benefits of cloud computing technology are that it provides access to a broader audience and pools computational muscle, bandwidth, and processing speed in a seamless fashion. Cloud computing technology must have something distinctive that makes it unique and identifiable. NIST strongly suggests that the phrase "cloud computing" be reserved but not limited to systems that have five essential characteristics. 12

[12] (Mell and Grance, 2012)

1. Scalable: It must be a flexible, scalable solution that can be scaled up or down, at any time.
2. Accessible: It must host ubiquitously available devices such as smartphones, personal data assistants, and various other computing platforms, and allow you to access your information from anywhere, and on any device.
3. Rapid Elasticity: Resources can be added to a network through the cloud without having to install and configure tests and validate additional servers.
4. Resource Driven: Computing resources can be pooled into a single location to serve all consumers using a multi-tenant model that can be dynamically assigned and reassigned on demand. The exact location of the provided resources need not be revealed.
5. Metered: A measured service for which you pay per use as resources are needed.

Service Models:

Cloud computing technology can conform to many different service models delivering a plethora of services. Cloud computing can be configured to provide many different types of services. These models include but are not limited to:

1. SaaS – Software as a Service: A delivery model in which software is provided and licensed across the Internet on a subscription basis and is centrally hosted and typically accessed by users using a device via a web browser.
2. PaaS – Platform as a Service: Is a model where customers can work online to develop, execute, and manage applications for launching an application.
3. IaaS – Infrastructure as a Service: Is the provisioning, processing, storage, and building of networks, and other virtualized computing resources over the Internet where the

user has control over operating systems, storage, and applications and can run arbitrary software, but has limited control over the underlying cloud physical infrastructure.

4. StaaS – Storage as a Service: Is a service model in which a service provider provides digital storage on their own infrastructure in which space is rented on a subscription basis over the Internet.

5. TaaS – Testing as a Service: Is the outsourcing of an area of testing to a service provider. Usually, this includes non-critical automated regression testing, performance testing, security testing, testing of software, and cloud-based applications.

6. SecaaS – Security as a Service: Involves the deployment of security applications such as anti-virus, logging, authentication, single sign-on, authorization, device profiling, encryption, alerting, malware detection/prevention over the Internet by an outside organization.

7. DaaS – Desktop as a Service: Is a virtual desktop infrastructure (VDI) in which the customer's personal data is copied to and from a virtual desktop that is independent of the user's location, device, and network. The VDI is managed by a third party who administers the back-end infrastructure.

8. MaaS – Monitoring/Management as a Service: Is a collection of information technology tools for gathering information regarding the applications and hardware operating at the client's location as well as supply activity reports. Monitoring provides remote tracking of network and computer health and to enhance the overall performance and management of the resources.

9. CaaS – Communication, Content, and Computing as a Service: Is the outsourcing of data, voice and video communications which include but is not limited to Voice over IP (VoIP or Internet telephony), Instant Messaging (IM), collaboration, video conference applications using fixed and mobile devices, etc.

10. IdaaS – Identity as a Service: Is an authentication infrastructure that is built, hosted and managed by a service provider for the cloud.
11. BaaS – Backup as a Service: Is the backup and recovery services managed by the outside provider.
12. AaaS – Application as a Service: Is an Application Service Provider that provides access to a particular software application over the Internet.
13. EaaS – Everything as a Service: Refers to "X as a service," "anything as a service" or "everything as a service." It is the variety of services and applications emerging for users to access on-demand over the Internet rather than provided locally or on-site. XaaS is the essence of cloud computing.

These models are merely a few of the standard terms used for services within the cloud community.

NIST Service Models

NIST provides a description for three distinct service models. Almost all of the services provided by cloud computing fit into these models:

Software as a Service (SaaS)

SaaS is where the Service Provider provides applications to the client over the Internet. Applications are accessible from various client devices through a thin client interface such as a web browser (e.g., web-based email). In this service model scenario, the consumer does not manage or control the underlying cloud infrastructure including network, servers, operating systems, storage, or critical configuration components. The user can change limited user-specific application configuration settings.

Platform as a Service (PaaS)

PaaS gives the client the ability to deploy onto the cloud infrastructure consumer-created or acquired applications created using programming languages and tools supported by the SP. The user does not manage or control the underlying cloud infrastructure including network, servers, operating systems, or storage, but has control over the deployed applications and possibly application hosting environment configurations.

Infrastructure as a Service (IaaS)

IaaS gives the client the ability to provision processing, storage, networks, and other fundamental computing resources where the consumer can deploy and run arbitrary software, which can include operating systems and applications. The user does not manage or control the underlying cloud infrastructure but has control over operating systems, storage, deployed applications, and possibly limited control of select networking components (e.g., host firewalls).

Deployment Models

Because cloud technology is a consistently evolving paradigm, it is hard to provide an exact definition for the many different variations in cloud deployment models. NIST references four types of deployment models. Most SPs have carved out their niche in the cloud computing business by catering their services around each of the four primary NIST deployment models. The general characteristics of the four types are:

Private Cloud

The private cloud infrastructure is operated solely for an organization. Private clouds can be managed by the community or by a third party. This type of cloud can be administrated on or off the premises.

Community Cloud

A community cloud infrastructure is one that is shared by several organizations. It supports a specific community that has shared concerns. Community clouds can be managed by the community or by a third party. This type of cloud has the option of being administrated on or off the premises.

Public Cloud

The public cloud infrastructure is made available to the public or as a large industry group. Public clouds are owned by organizations who sell cloud services.

Hybrid Cloud

The hybrid cloud infrastructure is a composition of two or more clouds (private, community, or public) that remain unique entities but are bound together by standardized or proprietary technology that enables the best practices from both deployment models. In this model, access can be provided to the community while certain aspects of the cloud can also be held private or public and private clouds can be leveraged to balance the load between clouds.

Some SPs have proprietary hybrid solutions that blend unique deployment models. These solutions are based on a business's organizational structure and location. Some proprietary solutions include storing critical records from the Documentation Control and Retention Department in a local private cloud while general non-critical information is stored in the public cloud. It is important to note that each deployment model should be designed for the type of information that is being handled. Each deployment model has its strengths and weaknesses. For example, a private cloud may not be the most cost-efficient deployment model, but it is preferred because it allows the exertion of additional control over the cloud security and provides distinct levels of privacy. Many regulated organizations in health care such as hospitals, private practices, outpatient services, home health care services or a host of other pharmaceutical companies, chemical companies, medical device companies, hospitals, biotechnology companies, etc. favor the private cloud deployment model because they can readily conform to regulatory standards.

From an organizational standpoint, the number one concern involving computer technology is the protection of regulated data. If your business's data is not in regulatory scope, then your computer systems do not require agency controls. Most companies do not believe that their practices are regulated and therefore do not put regulatory controls in place. However, well over ninety percent of businesses produce information that is governed by a number of different government initiatives. Experienced computer experts implement necessary controls to ensure compliance with government regulations. Mature organizations rely on technical, procedural, organizational, and administrative controls to meet regulatory requirements.

Companies, regulatory agencies, and consumers play a vital role in manufacturing, monitoring, and ensuring products and services are safe. Where the confusion lies is in how safety is perceived and at what point and to what degree security should be implemented to keep information secure. Each entity involved in providing quality products and service may see data protection differently and believe that appropriate resources should be applied to protect their interest.

- From a business perspective, the priority of security surrounding data protection for computer systems would likely be system intellectual property, personal data protection, and national security.
- From the consumer's perspective, the priority of security surrounding data protection for computer systems would be personal protection, system security, and national security.

- From a government perspective, the priority of security surrounding data protection for computer systems is that national security trumps all the other directives. In times of peril and conflict, national security directives are primary directives.

Leveraging the cloud to cut capital expenditure and control operating costs makes it an ideal solution for your business. It is important to understand the various deployment models available on the cloud. There are many different variations in cloud deployment models. The question is which deployment model should be taken into consideration for your design and what are the risks of not conforming to a particular layout. It is important that the deployment model runs parallel with your business objectives.

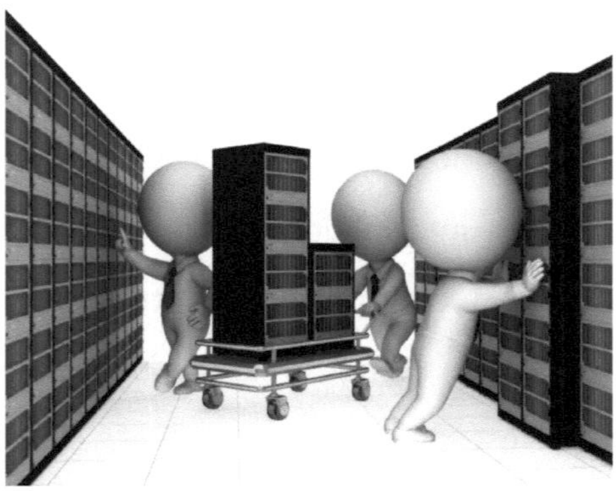

Each deployment model should be designed around the type of information that is being handled. Because cloud technology is consistently evolving, it 's hard to pinpoint all of the variations involved in cloud deployment models. This book cannot explain them all because cloud technology is constantly changing. Some CSPs have proprietary hybrid solutions that blend unique deployment models by providing a solution based on a business's organizational structure and alternative locations. It is important to note that each deployment model should be designed about the type of information that is being handled. Nevertheless, most SPs have carved out their niche in the cloud computing business by focusing their services on one of the four primary NIST service models.

Cloud computing is a means to an end. NIST's description of deployment models, service models, and essential characteristics originated to help develop the first steps in the growth of cloud deployment models. The characterization helps us conceptualize a baseline and serves as a method for comparing cloud services and deployment strategies. Deployment models should complement industry objectives. Deployment, characteristics, and services should be solutions to broader business goals. Access to an extended application, platform, and infrastructure as a service is simply a means to address specific business needs. If a deployment model does not satisfy the requirements for security and privacy, data controls, access, data types, typology, integrity, statutory compliance, trade, and governance, etc., then that business could be throwing resources into the wind. Choosing wrong deployment models can stifle employees, hamper creativity and choke businesses. There is nothing worse than having a cloud solution that is not aligned with business objectives. Business IT solutions are not necessarily situated in one deployment model. Many companies are developing hybrid cloud solutions that contain a plethora of solution-based services.

FDA Information Management (IM) Strategic Plan

The Food and Drug Administration (FDA or Agency) is one of the most information-intensive regulatory agencies in the world. The FDA operates on many continents across the globe. Like most corporations, the FDA is managed through information and distinct processes. Most people think that the FDA's responsibility is limited to ensuring the effectiveness, quality, purity, and safety of food and drug products and services in the US, but do not realize that it operates a complex data information repository in many continents across the globe. Like a living organism, the FDA is constantly growing and ever evolving. It houses one of the largest data knowledge and operations repositories in the world. To have a global presence, it is necessary to establish a hybrid cloud system that complements the agency's activities. Having access to high quality, high availability, high performing data networks, and servers and application infrastructure is an essential requirement for establishing communication services that can be accessed from computer applications, and mobile devices anywhere in the world. Internal workforce capabilities are critical to the FDA's operations, as well as for the integrity of connectivity to the public. Building a private architecture that exhibits real-time connectivity with real-time metrics captured with the major performance indicators (KPIs), dashboards, scorecards, and wireframes is the only way to manage analytics for an ever-expanding repository. It helps in the understanding of each community.

The FDA has decided to reap the benefits of cloud services. It has developed a private cloud solution for managing its disaster recovery activities.13 Currently, the full recovery time for FDA cloud computing resources in the event of a catastrophe is within 45 minutes of discovery. In the case of a virus attack and server failure, data can be restored onto additional configured servers in their environment. The private cloud infrastructure has been developed by the FDA and has been used solely by its organization. No third parties were involved in developing solutions. A senior tech adviser at the FDA said;

> *"An internal cloud approach means that we do not have to pay for costly service contracts with outsourcers, nor do we have to dedicate rooms full of servers to sit idly by just in case of a serious problem."*

[13] (FDA, 2015)

Historically, companies that operate in a non-cloud environment would in some cases duplicate dedicated servers as back-ups or use valuable outsourced services. The FDA has decided to develop an internal cloud computing disaster recovery approach. This approach allows the agency to backup or restore data in a fraction of the time.

The FDA has many goals for their new data center. One of these goals includes modernizing technology and infrastructure to construct a cloud computing data center that is secure, scalable, elastic, reliable and includes extensive virtualization. An outcome of this initiative has yielded the FDA's first state-of-the-art production data center environment. The new data center gives the FDA the ability to host mission critical servers and computer systems, with fully redundant subsystems (cooling, power, network links, storage, etc.) and compartmentalizes security zones, which are controlled by biometric access control methods. The production data center is inherently less prone to failures due to its fully fault-tolerant cooling, power and network links engineered to exceed 99.995% availability. The FDA proclaims that it will yield less than twenty-seven minutes of downtime per year. The FDA has achieved operational efficiency and cost savings by consolidating servers and virtualizing the environment.

The operational efficiencies include an 89% server reduction through virtualization and a decrease in the number of agency systems. Unlike before, the FDA can run multiple systems on a single high-performance server. The system no longer requires a separate server. Virtualization allows the FDA to reduce the physical server footprint, which demonstrates savings in power consumption costs from a server and data center standpoint. Also, it allows the FDA to utilize equipment and support resources far more efficiently. Some database servers have been consolidated since the onset of cloud service.

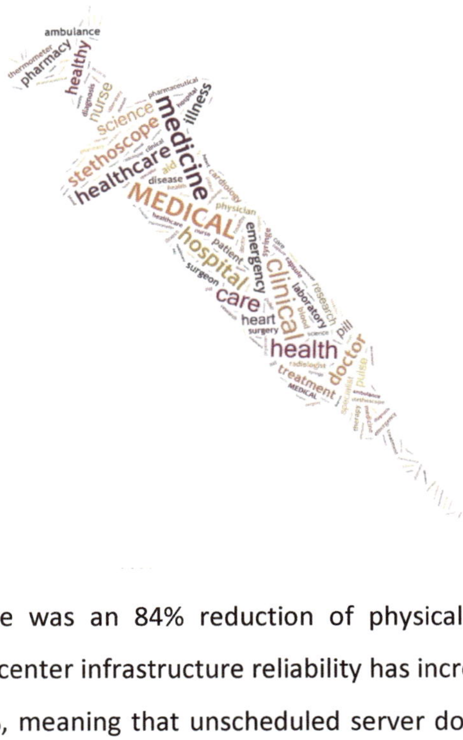

There was an 84% reduction of physical equipment. The overall data center infrastructure reliability has increased from 98.3% to 99.9996%, meaning that unscheduled server downtime has been reduced from 6.6 days per calendar year to approximately 30 seconds. The data center consolidations, coupled with forgoing future investments, have saved the FDA $19,706,000.

European Cloud Computing Initiative

The European Union (EU) Commission states that everyone has the right to personal data protection. Whether a person is home watching cable TV, at work on the computer, or at school composing a paper, their electronic fingerprints must be protected. The EU charter states that data protection is a fundamental right, and this right extends to all aspects of life.14

Computer experts must understand that in the EU, everyone has the right to be forgotten. In other words, European data protection rules protect data by enforcing the right to be forgotten. Personal identifying information must not be linked back to a particular person or reside on the network without your permission.

[14] (|, Ferraro, and Carmona, 2015)

Housed data must not be indirectly or directly affiliated with identifying characteristics that are associated with a person. Identifying characteristics include any economic, emotional, behavioral, physical, or social stigmas related to a particular person. It is not merely physical information that's protected, but also any personal data, that indirectly describes a person's conditions or attributes, otherwise known as "a state of being" is protected under EU law.

Data retrieved from various personalized data such as bank accounts, medical records, occupational descriptions, Social Security numbers, photographs, addresses (email or URL), and more that's accessed through various methods, must not linger as fragmented information that's floating around in some computer system. Computer systems, PDAs (Personal Digital Assistants), telephones, emails, websites, IP (internal protocol) addresses, and more are susceptible to penetration or infiltration and must be included in a plan to be deleted.

SPs must design their environment to delete personal data from companies, corporations, and private owners who no longer want data to be processed. Data protection must be seamlessly built into a cloud computing framework. If personal data is not deleted, holders of the data must be explicitly informed about why their data must be kept. Each entity that consumes data must clearly state to the data owner what information is owned. If foreign companies offer goods or services in the EU or monitor the online behavior of citizens, they are responsible for following data protection rules. Data protection rules are not designed to address the individual requirement for handling personal information. EU data protection rules are intended to create a foundation and general approach for providing data handling standards at the national level. Also, companies must actualize a plan for data breaches.

Today's cloud environment is continuously changing. Cloud applications store and share all types of data. Employees and customers are sharing more information than ever before. Employees transport and store personal information on company devices and company information on personal devices. Enforcing data protection in the cloud has become a complex task. It is an ever-evolving security threat that has piqued companies' awareness. Email addresses, phone numbers, employee Social Security numbers, medical histories, credit card numbers, spouse information, billing addresses, birth dates, insurance information, etc., are in the cloud.

Small businesses should reassess their security plans to protect themselves against cyber-attacks and malware. The EU has developed data protection rules. They have also enforced a data protection authority to hear cases involving these rules.15 Each EU participating country has their data protection regulations for processing data protection violations. The EU provides overarching data protection rules with increased responsibility and accountability for those processing confidential, and private data. Confidential or personal information shared with a psychologist, attorney, physician, or therapist must not be divulged to third parties without the express consent of the client. Private data must be free from intrusion into one's personal matters, and personal information privacy is a right rooted in common law.

The European Commission, the executive arm of the EU, believes that cloud computing is the game changer they have been waiting for. The European Commission has determined that cloud computing has the potential to unleash millions of dollars into the economy. The commission has outlined bold initiatives that are expected to deliver millions of European jobs. Cloud computing technology is expected to provide an annual boost to the European economy of approximately €160 billion. The European Commission expects cloud computing to grow the European Gross Domestic Product (GDP) by roughly 1% by 2020.16

---

[15] (Metheny, M. (2013) Federal cloud computing)
[16] (COMM, 2016)

The commission's strategy is incredibly ambitious. The approach consists of a multi-prong strategy. The plan is to deploy cloud computing technologies across member nations. The Commission believes that the best way to integrate cloud computing technology into the EU framework is by leveraging the expertise of academia and think tanks combined with the financial wherewithal of the private sector and the implementation of new policies and laws from the government. This entwined relationship is expected to drive creativity, integration, and acceptance of the technology along with establishing a level of trusted certification, interoperability, and collaboration.

The European Commission believes that the stakeholders are best suited to operate and manage cloud technologies. If stakeholders can profit from this new technology, it will grow on its own. In return, the European Commission won't have to pour money into monitoring its growth but will have minimal oversight. The

European Commission can focus on ensuring accountability for privacy laws and SLAs. This relationship will give the commission the tools it needs to generate taxable income for managing cloud technologies. Stakeholders, not the EU, will have a vested interest in the availability and the types of technologies being metered in the cloud environment. It is the stakeholders who will determine what services will be successful in the cloud environment because they can determine what services are profitable. The commission's equation has calculated that profitability means success. Governments can tax the success. It is assumed that demand for services such as online music and movie streaming, online banking, education, social networking services, and web-based email will drive profitability.

The European Commission's goal is to utilize key stakeholders and potential investors to unleash the potential of cloud computing in Europe.17 People, businesses, and institutions that want to take the risk can reap the profits from this huge economic windfall. As part of the new strategy to drive European business and government productivity via cloud computing, the European Commission has defined cloud computing as:

> *'Cloud computing' refers to the storage of data (such as text files, pictures and video) and software on remote computers, which users access over the internet on the device of their choice. This is faster, cheaper, more*

[17] (COMM, 2016b)

flexible and potentially more secure than on-site IT solutions.[18]

The European Commission understands the potential impact that cloud computing can have on their economy and the benefits of making computer technology secure, scalable, elastic, reliable, available, faster, and cheaper. Cloud computing has the potential to change the way Europeans operate their business and conduct services within their businesses. Companies can determine the way in which their services are being delivered. Stakeholders can offer a unique mix of product and services and, thus, win big. The commission is encouraging interested parties and investors to step up to the plate, make the initial investment and take ownership of this economic windfall. The European Commission plans to support stakeholders by working through a myriad of regulations and establishing laws and policies that enhance growth and achieve meaningful infrastructure changes that facilitate a host of cloud-based products and services.

Trying to create a path towards EU acceptance of cloud computing, for all of its members, can be extremely challenging. The European Commission is taking measures to understand better the technical and social challenges that may be inhibiting companies from entering into this new phenomenon. There are a lot of unrealized legal challenges surrounding cloud computing in the European region. The European Commission is committed to

---

[18] (COMM, 2012)

removing any regional challenges inhibiting the growth of cloud computing and to strengthening regulations surrounding data compliance, data protection and portability, copyright laws, geographical restrictions, etc. The cloud architecture must be designed such that European privacy laws are not violated. Procedural controls, technical controls, administrative controls, and organizational structure all play a role in ensuring the transparency, confidentiality integrity, and availability of personal information.

However, not everyone believes that the new privacy laws will achieve cloud growth. Many entities feel that EU laws governing data privacy and restrictions on cloud integration are far more restrictive than those in the US. It is believed that the EU initiative governing privacy challenges the open cloud concept. It restricts hybrid solutions that circumvent the legal framework by creating illusive data paths. Nevertheless, when designing an appropriate deployment model, EU laws governing data privacy and developing a cloud typology must be considered.

The magnitude of services being offered in the cloud is unimaginable. Communities are mesmerized by it, and it continues to challenge our curiosity. The cloud phenomenon is not limited to individuals or any one European region, but it has the profound effect on the way we do business and how we live. Cloud computing is integrated into the fabric of Europeans' lives. It has an unseen grasp on all aspects of European existence. Businesses use it to make their processes more efficient. Consumers want to try and enjoy different technologies. Governments want to simplify cloud infrastructure by deconstructing delivery of services for ease of taxing cloud technologies at specific operational nodes. The challenge for the EU is ensuring that privacy laws are not violated as data flows from one jurisdiction to another. Who has control over that data? Where is the data processed, stored, and what security and privacy arrangements have been made? What technical, regulatory, privacy and security requirements must be met? Should the location where the data originated be held responsible for meeting all of the requirements, or should the EU establish a set of overarching laws and data standards?

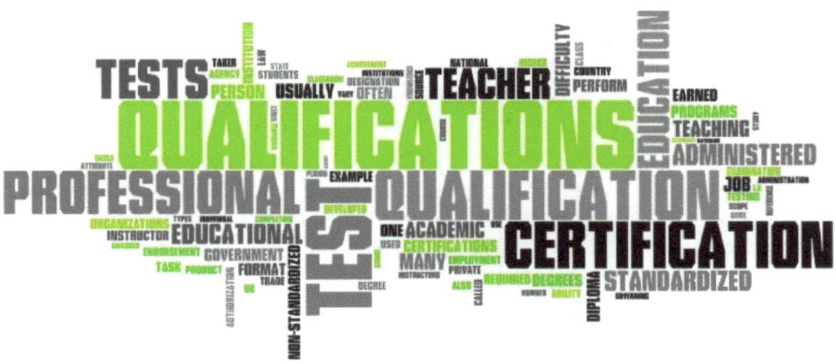

EU Technical Standards

Technical standards inhibit the acceptance of cloud computing technology in Europe. Having different technical standards for each European region will affect how IT environments interoperate. Suppose you decide to move an application between clouds. Some challenges might be that the target cloud:

1. Must be able to support the application

2. Must not change the application's functionality
3. Must retain the same security controls
4. Must be able to rebuild the application stack
5. Must be able to manipulate encrypted data

The software application must be able to interoperate between clouds. Interoperation is essential for the acceptance of the cloud computing technology. Without collaboration among member states to encourage interoperability among cloud networks, cloud development would virtually come to a complete stop. The flow of investments into cloud technology would trickle.

The EU officially recognizes the European Telecommunications Standards Institute (ETSI) as a major player in shaping technical standards.19 ETSI produces globally-applicable standards for Information and Communications Technologies (ICT), including fixed, mobile, radio, converged, broadcast and Internet technologies. ETSI also provides quality of service metrics and monitoring capabilities that aid in determining the effectiveness of cloud communication services. Quality services, such as speed, accuracy, availability, reliability, security, simplicity, flexibility, capability, usability, fidelity, etc., are a crucial part of the cloud experience lifecycle. The European Commission has made it a priority to streamline and reduce the red tape behind the acceptance of standards that govern the quality of service of Europeans' cloud computing experience. Developing a set of quality of service metrics that can be used as the gold standard for measuring cloud

[19] (2016, 2017)

capabilities would help standardize performance expectations for all European nations.

In the cloud, deployment models, characteristics, and cloud services consist of a host of interoperating elements. These features range from small devices up to supercomputers. The elements serve individuals, multinational corporations, and global communities.

Each entity participates in the service of data, information, and knowledge to and from every country in the world. To reduce the red tape behind the regional member states' acceptance of cloud standards, the European Commission aims to conduct front-end research to identify technical complexities and legal conflict among countries. It is their belief that by identifying and reducing the complexities behind technical standards, greater interoperability, data portability, and security will be achieved.

The acceptance of technical standards allows users across the EU to normalize their communication backbone. It sets a level of expectation for everyone within the European cloud community.

Establishing requirements for speed, accuracy, availability, reliability, security, simplicity, flexibility, capability, usability, fidelity, etc. gives investors and developers the confidence that certain products and services will perform as expected. Developers can align their products and services around network capabilities. There is no benefit in providing online gaming to a community whose network is incapable of processing it.

Certification Programs

The European Commission is also encouraging certification. Certification must be established for the stakeholders to discern the trustworthiness of the cloud environment. Data is transported across huge distances, from one cloud provider to another, utilizing various technologies. It is imperative that integrity is verified through certification. The European Commission believes that development and recognition for EU-wide certification programs for the trustworthiness of cloud providers are essential for growing their industry.

The EU continues to promote a legal structure that requires certification of cloud service providers. The EU is working towards providing a legal framework that would require certification of cloud service providers. Eventually, it will be a prerequisite for SPs to substantiate specific industry standards and safeguards to ensure the quality of data. Certification and SLAs measure the trustworthiness of the process and ensure that cloud service providers are complying with their obligations.

Creating an environment for investigating technical standards, SLAs, and certifications lay the groundwork that will establish a compliant cloud computing environment. By planting the seeds for the start-up compliance, the hope is that this effort will empower regulatory authorities to create certifying bodies. These administrators can identify and flush out SPs that are not living up to the requirements contained in theSLA, and that are not providing an expected quality of service. Trust is at the heart of the cloud experience. The European Commission believes that the SP will certify that they are abiding by the standards that are required. Certifications are at the core of that faith. SPs must comply with legal obligations and must be certified.

The European Commission believes that transparency with stakeholders will aid in the promotion of trusted cloud sources. Certification will also allow the mapping of similar technical specifications and create a framework across the global environment. Thus, increasing the interoperability of cloud technologies will automatically mature scalability requirements. Certification will allow regulating bodies to adopt standards for which to guide and promote cloud activities and create a baseline of performance metrics on which cloud service providers can operate. Europeans are expected to rely on certifying bodies to determine the trustworthiness of the cloud service provider. In addition to SLAs and certification, CSPs must comply with legal audit requirements for applications and systems. CSPs must submit to governance and oversight to ensure reliability and trustworthiness.

Service level agreements

The European Commission's model for cloud computing revolves around the SLA between the SP and the European Commission.20 Development of quality expectations and fair contract terms are the basis for establishing hosting arrangements between the contract service provider and the European Commission. During the certification period, the contract service provider must provide the European Commission with evidence from a test that has evaluated the quality of service. With the explosion of the cloud environment and the plethora of new technologies, there

[20] (*52015DC0192 - EN - EUR-Lex*, 2016)

is no better way to control the interaction and collaboration among SPs than with theSLA.

The SLA is a legally binding negotiated document that sets real expectations for services that are offered to the customer. Expectations for speed, accuracy, availability, reliability, security, simplicity, flexibility, capability, usability, and fidelity should be discussed in the contract. The best cloud services are the ones that have their obligations verified in writing and are capable of being measured. Because the environment is in continuous flux, the SLA is the only way of determining a Quality of Service along with guaranteeing privacy and protection. The European Commission is the progenitor of cloud products and services across the EU. However, they also view themselves as the end client of the offered service. The SLA is in place for the duration of the contract and should include but not be limited to specifics surrounding:

1. Response Time: A mechanism should be put in place to determine how many users can concurrently use the service for a given period.
2. Programmed and Unexpected Downtime: Notifications for downtime and interruptions (such as sabotage, natural disasters, and unforeseen events) as well as maintenance should be communicated to the European Commission over a defined period.
3. Availability of Services: Content Service Providers must determine the length of time in which applications are available to users. The availability, rate and cost of the measurement period must be part of the metrics.
4. Monthly Hosting Reports: A monthly report covered in the above descriptions is to be submitted to the commission.

The European Commission would like the SLA to serve as a starting point for defining engineering and operational commitments. The service level specifications implemented by the Commission examine mechanisms placed by service level management, service level enforcement, as well as standard language and modeling.

The European Commission considers the SLAs to be a tool for gauging the quality and the type of service. This reasoning accrues because of the agreement between the SP and the European Commission. The SLA is a contract that provides an agreement for services that are approved by both parties. The agreement is predicated on establishing ongoing internal metrics that determine the quality of service.

The EU can provide metrics to organizations so that they can differentiate mediocre SPs from those that have a competitive edge. Developing an SLA lifecycle will help the commission to gauge cloud capabilities better while developing a policy that will better implement cloud computing technology. Cloud systems provide a plethora of new technologies and services. Most services being offered in the cloud have never used this mode of delivery. Standard expectations will aid in developing new technologies that are offered on-demand. With providers, brokers, customers, etc., the best way to monitor expectations, objectives, challenges, and usage patterns within the ecosystem is to implement SLAs. The Commission believes that SLAs are the way to establish:

1. Goals through Quality of Service (QoS).
2. Privacy and protection constraints through Quality of Protection (QoP).
3. Expectations through the description of actions. According to the QoS, this is a necessity to deliver the service.
4. Responsibilities through the inclusion of obligations of parties including penalties and exclusion terms.
5. Evolvement cases through the definition of rules that enable efficient adaptation of resource provisioning based on the changing demands of the applications and the end users.

Partnership

The European Commission is not in the business of purchasing and managing a publicly run data center. Nor does it propel a particular architecture for deployment models, service models, or force design characteristics down the throats of European consumers. Cloud stakeholders fundamentally determine how IT is delivered and consumed. The purpose of the partnership is to combine resources, expertise suppliers, and vendors so that the conversation begins.

> *"Cloud computing is a game-changer for our economy. Without EU action, we will stay stuck in national fortresses and miss out on billions in economic gains. We must achieve critical mass and a single set of rules across Europe. We must tackle the perceived risks of cloud computing head-on."*

The European Commission is inviting public authorities and industry leaders, cloud buyers, and technology suppliers into a European cloud partnership. As stated before, this partnership is responsible for establishing cloud standards. These standards include, but are not limited to, security, interoperability, and procurement. The Commission would like these partners to provide criteria for performance, design, functional specifications, and architecture of the cloud.

> *"Europe needs to think big. The cloud strategy will enhance trust in innovative computing solutions and boost a competitive digital single market where Europeans feel safe. That means a swift adoption of the new data protection framework which the Commission proposed earlier this year and the development of safe and fair contract terms and conditions."*

Cloud computing is an ever evolving long-term paradigm. Most people do not understand the capabilities nor its limitations. Its existence has forged the emergence of new technologies and services. This cyber technology supplants a previous generation of old centralized IT processing models. Cloud computing has helped us move away from a centralized computing model, where the user is the manager, to a place where everything is managed by someone else. The European Commission does not want to impose their vision of cloud computing technology but would like to spur communication between the public and the private sector. This communication will hopefully create an environment where technology providers will engage with business partners, vendors, users, customers, and CSPs in ways never seen before. Cloud computing can soar. The growth and profitability of cloud computing are best monitored through SLAs. SLAs govern how CSPs interact with the public and private sector and regulate provisioning, collaboration, and interaction by defining the terms of engagement for participating entities. It is easy to define deployment models, characteristics, and services the cloud provides, but there is more than meets the eye than what is in the definition.

Bibliography

1. 2016, E. (2017) *European telecommunications standards institute*. Available at: http://www.etsi.org/

2. *52015DC0192 - EN - EUR-Lex* (2016) Available at: http://eur-lex.europa.eu/legal-content/EN/TXT/?uri=CELEX%3A52015DC0192

3. COMM (2012) European commission - PRESS RELEASES - press release - digital agenda: New strategy to drive European business and government productivity via cloud computing. Available at: http://europa.eu/rapid/press-release_IP-12-1025_en.htm

4. COMM (2016a) *European cloud strategy 2012*. Available at: https://ec.europa.eu/digital-single-market/en/european-cloud-computing-strategy

5. COMM (2016b) *European cloud strategy 2012*. Available at: https://ec.europa.eu/digital-single-market/en/european-cloud-computing-strategy

6. Department of Homeland Security, Office of the Chief Procurement Officer (2015) *Security authorization process guide version 11.1*. Available at: https://www.dhs.gov/sites/default/files/publications/Security%20Authorization%20Process%20Guide_v11_1.pdf

7. *EXHIBIT 300 CAPITAL ASSET PLAN AND BUSINESS CASE SUMMARY* (no date) Available at: https://www.gsa.gov/graphics/staffoffices/300ioi.pdf

8. FDA (2015) *Information technology strategic plan 2015-2018*. Available at: http://www.fda.gov/downloads/AboutFDA/ReportsManualsForms/Reports/UCM325437.pdf

9. Hawes, K. (2016) *What ITL does*. Available at: https://www.nist.gov/itl/about-itl

10. Joseph, J., Fellenstein, C. and Moss, G.L. (2003) *Grid computing*. United States: Prentice Hall.

11. KellyJOlson (2011) Available at: https://www.gsa.gov/graphics/staffoffices/FY2011OCSITAnnualReport.pdf

12. Lutchman, R. (2003) Computerized work management systems for utility and plant operations. Lancaster, PA: DEStech Publications.

13. Matloff, N. (2015) Parallel computing for data science: With examples in R, C++ and Cuda. Boca Raton, FL, United States: CRC Press.

14. Mell, P. and Grance, T. (2012) The NIST definition of cloud computing recommendations of the national institute of standards and technology special publication 800-145. Available at: http://nvlpubs.nist.gov/nistpubs/Legacy/SP/nistspecialpublication800-145.pdf

15. Metheny, M. (2013) Federal cloud computing: The definitive guide for cloud service providers. New York, NY, United States: Syngress Publishing.

16. OMB (2008) *REPORT TO CONGRESS ON THE BENEFITS OF THE PRESIDENT'S E-GOVERNMENT INITIATIVES*. Available at: https://www.whitehouse.gov/sites/default/files/omb/assets/egov_docs/FY08_Benefits_Report.pdf

17. *Program overview* (no date) Available at: https://www.fedramp.gov/about-us/about/

18. *S. Rept. 113-157 - THE FEDERAL DATA CENTER CONSOLIDATION ACT OF 2013* (no date) Available at: https://www.congress.gov/congressional-report/113th-congress/senate-report/157/1

19. Schlosser, L., Member, B., Peter Tseronis, DOE, Peter Mell, NIST and for ISPAB (2009) *Federal cloud computing governance framework*. Available at: http://csrc.nist.gov/groups/SMA/ispab/documents/minutes/2009-12/cloud-computing-government-tic.pdf

20. YOUR RIGHTS AS A DATA SUBJECT WHAT CAN YOU DO IF YOUR RIGHTS ARE VIOLATED DATA TRANSFERS TO NON-EU COUNTRIES USEFUL ADDRESSES AND NUMBERS (no date) Available at:

http://ec.europa.eu/justice/policies/privacy/docs/guide/guide-ukingdom_en.pdf

21. |, E., Ferraro, F. and Carmona, J. (2015) *IN-DEPTH ANALYSIS*. Available at: http://www.europarl.europa.eu/RegData/etudes/IDAN/2015/554168/EPRS_IDA(2015)554168_EN.pdf